Wonders

McGraw Hill Education

Cover and Title Page: Nathan Love

www.mheonline.com/readingwonders

Mc Graw Hill

Copyright © 2017 McGraw-Hill Education

Send all inquiries to:
McGraw-Hill Education
2 Penn Plaza
New York, NY 10121

ISBN: 978-0-02-132473-6
MHID: 0-02-132473-5

Printed in the United States of America.

6 7 8 9 MER 28 27 26 25 24   C

Wonders

ELD
Companion Worktext

Program Authors

Diane August

Jana Echevarria

Josefina V. Tinajero

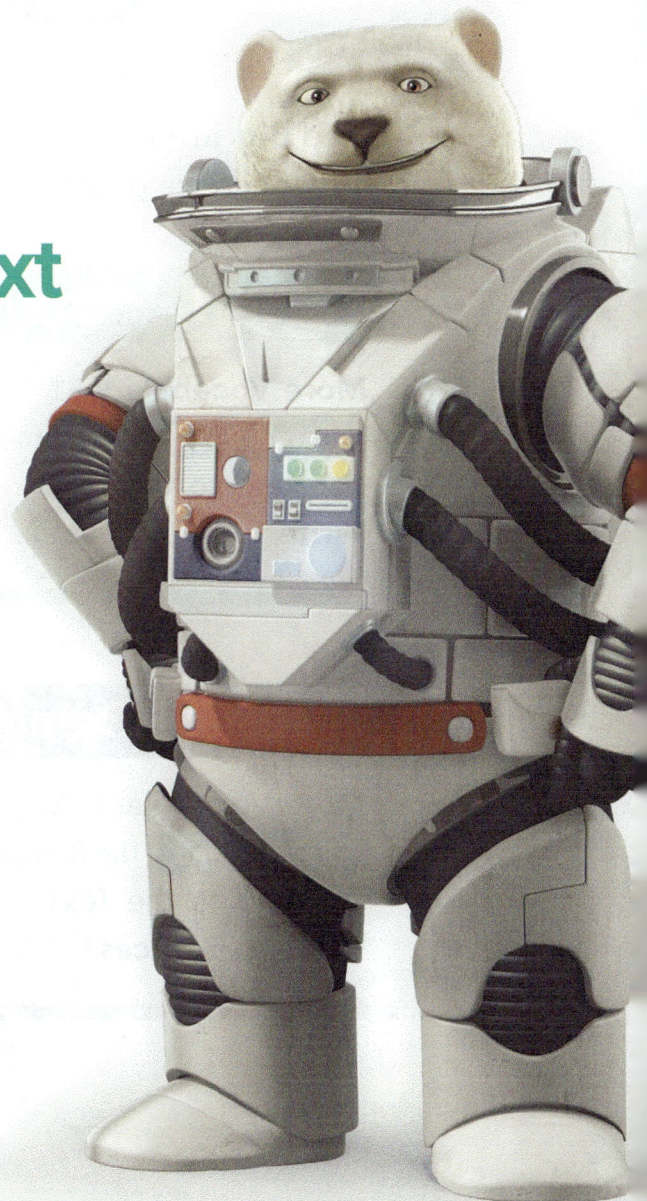

McGraw Hill Education

Excursions Across Time

The Big Idea

Socrates

Excursions Across Time

The Big Idea

What can we gain from reading about past civilizations?

? Essential Question

What contributions were made by early civilizations?

>> *Go Digital*

Look at the stone columns. What skills did the builders need to make them? Write the skills in the chart.

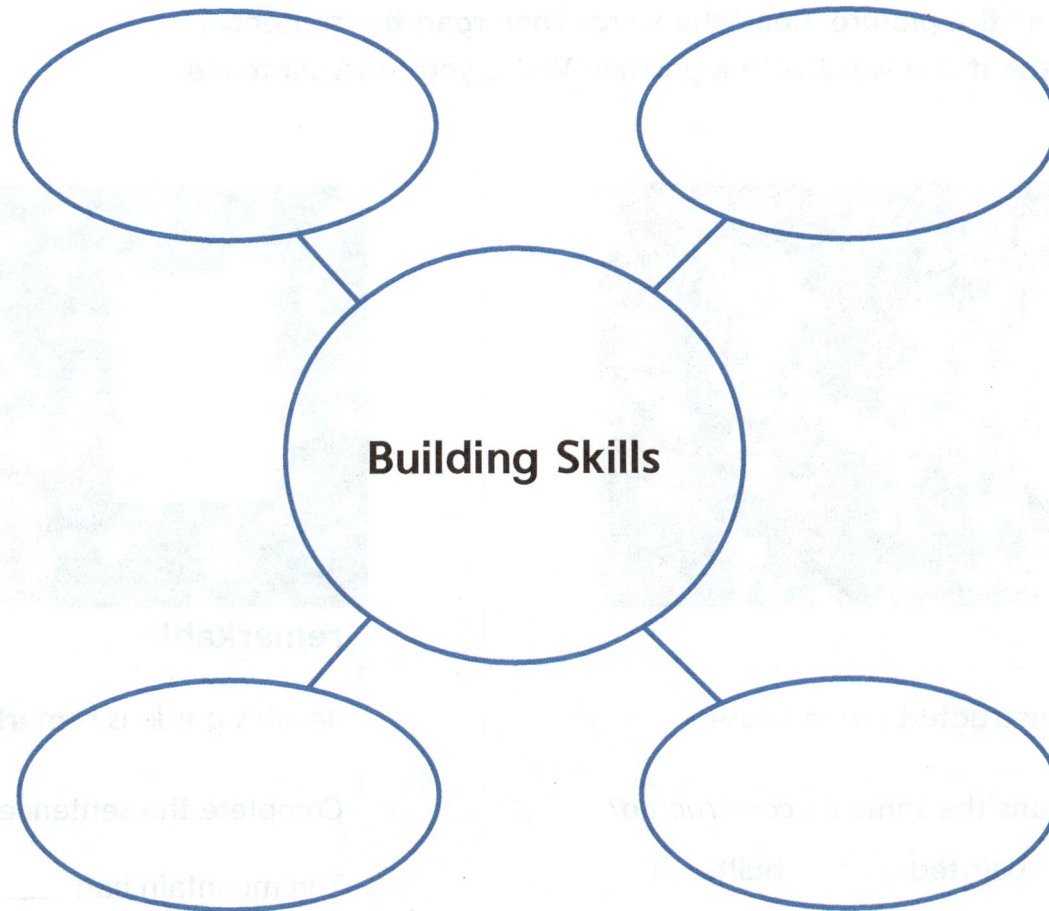

Building Skills

Discuss the skills the builders needed. Use words from the chart. Complete the sentences.

The builders needed to _____ the stone. They needed to make

the _____. They needed to _____ the

pictures. They needed to _____ the columns.

More Vocabulary

Look at the picture. Read the word. Then read the sentence. Talk about the word with a partner. Write your own sentence.

constructed

The children **constructed** a tree house.

What word means the same as *constructed*?

climbed   painted   built

What have you constructed?

I have constructed _____

_____.

remarkable

Jacob's grade is **remarkable**.

Complete the sentence. Write the word.

The mountain had _____ views.

What is one remarkable place you have seen?

One remarkable place I have seen

is _____.

Words and Phrases: Multiple-Meaning Words

The word *key* means "a tool to open a lock."

What does a key do?

A **key** opens locks.

The word *key* also means "important."

What is the boy doing?

He is writing the **key** ideas in his notebook.

COLLABORATE Talk with a partner. Look at the pictures. Read the sentences. Underline the correct meaning of the word *key*.

Sandra makes many *key* decisions.

tool to open a lock   **important**

The boy used his *key*.

tool to open a lock   **important**

COLLABORATE

❶ Talk About It

Look at the photograph. Read the title. Discuss what you see. Use these words.

ship   **ancient**   **empire**   **sea**

Write about what you see.

The text is about _____

_____.

What do you notice about the ship in the photo?

The ship is _____

_____.

Take notes as you read the text.

Empire of the Sea

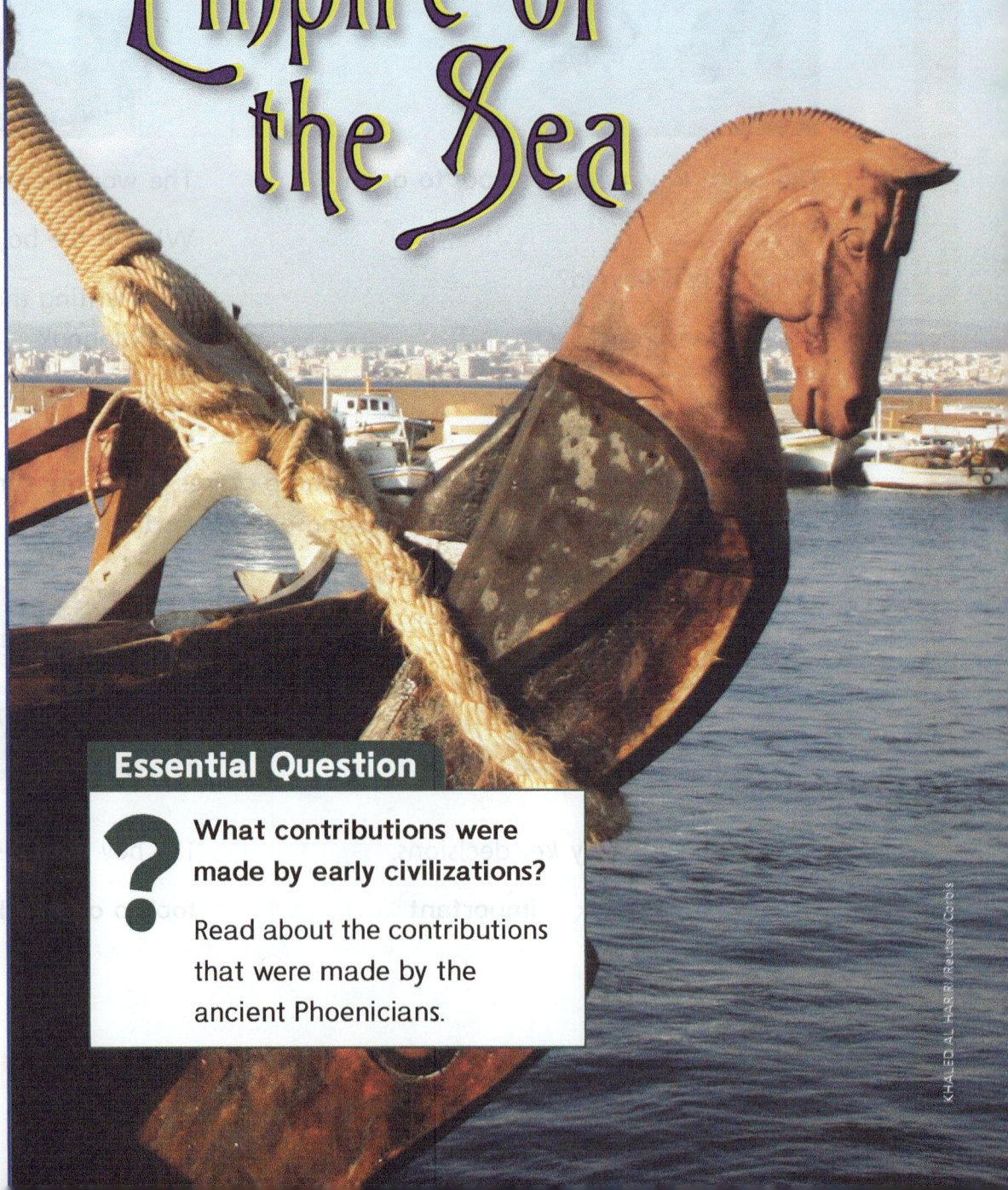

Essential Question

? **What contributions were made by early civilizations?**

Read about the contributions that were made by the ancient Phoenicians.

KHALED AL-HARIRI/Reuters/Corbis

Between the Mountains and the Sea

Around 1500 B.C., a **remarkable** civilization began to develop. Tiny Phoenicia was located between the Mediterranean Sea and the mountains. It would flourish for more than a millennium, or 1,000 years.

The Phoenicians would explore far beyond their homeland and establish a trading empire. They would thrive by finding clever solutions to key problems.

Resource Rich

Phoenicia was a small country, but it was rich in resources. Farmers grew many crops, including grapes, olives, and wheat. Cedar trees covered the hills. The Phoenicians had more resources than they needed to survive.

The Phoenicians used their resources to produce various goods. They cut cedar trees to build houses and other things. They used snail shells to make a special purple dye. They made beautiful objects out of glass. The Phoenicians wanted to find buyers for all of these goods and resources.

From Cedar Trees to Cargo Ships

The Phoenicians wanted to trade with their neighbors. These neighbors included the Greeks, the Egyptians, and the Hebrews. The best way to move their goods was across the Mediterranean Sea. But the Phoenician merchants had small boats that could not hold much cargo.

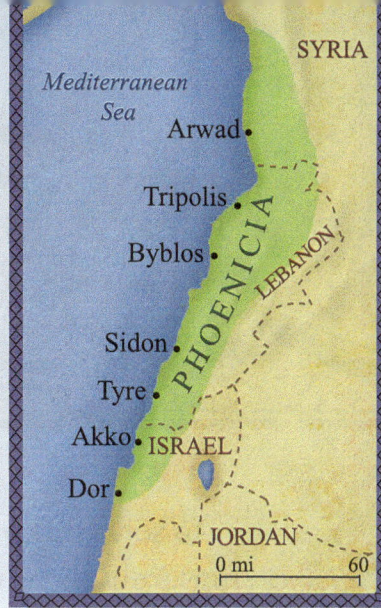

SYRIA

Mediterranean Sea

Arwad

Tripolis

Byblos

Sidon

Tyre

Akko · ISRAEL

Dor

PHOENICIA

LEBANON

JORDAN

0 mi 60

Text Evidence

1 Sentence Structure A C T

Read the first sentence of the second paragraph. Circle the word *and*. The word *and* connects two actions in the sentence. Draw a box around the two actions.

2 Specific Vocabulary A C T

Reread the first sentence of the second paragraph. The word *beyond* means "outside the limits of something." What did the Phoenicians go beyond? Write the word or words.

_____

3 Comprehension

Problem and Solution

Read "Resource Rich." The Phoenicians had many resources. Underline the sentence that explains the problem connected to this fact.

9

Text Evidence

1 Comprehension

Problem and Solution

Read the first paragraph. Phoenician boats couldn't hold much cargo. How did the Phoenicians solve this problem? Underline the sentence that tells you.

2 Specific Vocabulary ACT

Reread the first paragraph. The word *stable* means "steady and not likely to move." Why was it important for Phoenician ships to be stable?

A stable ship had to _____

_____.

COLLABORATE

3 Talk About It

How did the Phoenician sailors navigate at night?

At night, the Phoenicians _____

_____.

◄ Modern shipbuilders reproduce the designs of Phoenician ships.

To solve this problem, the Phoenicians **constructed** huge cargo ships from cedar wood. Construction began with a large wooden beam in the middle of the ship. Then they built a curved frame around the beam. The strong beam and curved frame kept the ship strong and stable in the water. Now the Phoenician ships could carry large, heavy loads.

The Phoenicians also became skilled navigators. In earlier times, traders had sailed only during the daytime. They stayed close to the coast. But the Phoenicians used the stars to find their way at night. They started by finding the North Star, which became known as the "Phoenician star."

Trade Routes and Trading Posts

The Phoenicians wanted to create a system of trade routes. But at the time, few routes were known. So the Phoenicians utilized their skills to develop their own routes. They traveled west and south around Africa. They traveled north to Europe. Phoenician routes helped other people trade, too. Some Phoenician ports, such as Carthage in North Africa, turned into big cities.

(t) KHALED AL HARIRI/Reuters/Corbis; (r) Album/Oronoz/Newscom

10

Timeline of Phoenician History

1300 B.C.
Phoenicians establish treaties with Egypt.

810 B.C.
The port city of Carthage is founded.

600 B.C.
Phoenicians sail as far as present-day Great Britain.

332 B.C.
The Greek army conquers the key Phoenician city of Tyre.

From Aleph to Zayin

Trade was going well. But the Phoenicians needed to keep records. Other people's writing systems were complicated. Egyptians used carved symbols called hieroglyphs. Mesopotamians used cuneiform, or shapes that represented letters and numbers. The Phoenicians wanted a simpler system.

They created an alphabet. Beginning with the letter *aleph*, the Phoenician alphabet included 22 consonants. Because of its simplicity, it was soon adopted in many places. It became the basis for alphabets used in many modern languages, including English.

By 300 B.C., the Phoenician civilization had begun to decline. But their alphabet, navigation, and ship designs lived on. Thousands of years later, the inventions of ancient Phoenicia continue to make our world better.

▲ The Phoenician alphabet used letters to represent sounds.

Make Connections

? Talk about the important contributions of the Phoenicians. **ESSENTIAL QUESTION**

Describe how one Phoenician innovation affects your everyday life. **TEXT TO SELF**

Text Evidence 🔍

❶ Specific Vocabulary Ⓐ Ⓒ Ⓣ

Read the first paragraph. A carved symbol is not written or drawn. It is cut into the surface of something. Why didn't the Phoenicians want to use carved symbols?

Using carved symbols was _____

_____.

❷ Sentence Structure Ⓐ Ⓒ Ⓣ

Read the first sentence of the second paragraph. Circle the pronoun. What noun phrase does this pronoun refer to?

This pronoun refers to _____.

❸ Comprehension
Problem and Solution

Reread the first paragraph. Circle one problem that the Phoenicians had. Then read the second paragraph. Write the solution to this problem.

The Phoenicians created _____

_____.

11

Respond to the Text

Partner Discussion Work with a partner. Read the questions about "Empire of the Sea." Show where you found text evidence. Write the page numbers. Then discuss what you learned.

How did the Phoenicians make ships better?

Before, _____.

The Phoenicians _____.

Text Evidence 🔍

Page(s): _____

Page(s): _____

How did the Phoenicians make navigation better?

Before, _____.

The Phoenicians _____.

Text Evidence 🔍

Page(s): _____

Page(s): _____

How did the Phoenicians make writing better?

Before, _____.

The Phoenicians _____.

Text Evidence 🔍

Page(s): _____

Page(s): _____

Group Discussion Present your answers to the group. Cite text evidence for your ideas. Listen to and discuss the group's opinions.

Write Work with a partner. Look at your notes about "Empire of the Sea." Write your answer to the Essential Question. Use text evidence to support your answer. Use vocabulary words in your writing.

What important changes did the Phoenicians make?

The Phoenicians made ships better by _____

_____.

The Phoenicians made navigation better by _____

_____.

The Phoenicians made writing better by _____

_____.

Share Writing Present your writing to the class. Discuss their opinions. Talk about their ideas. Explain why you agree or disagree with their ideas. You can say:

I agree with _____.

That's a good comment, but _____.

Write to Sources

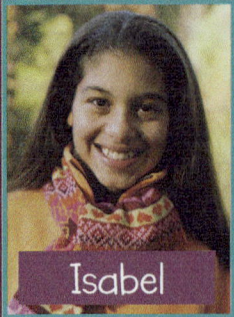

Isabel

Take Notes About the Text I took notes on the idea web to answer the prompt: *Describe a usual day in Carthage during the time of the Phoenicians. Use sensory details.*

Detail
Phoenician cargo ships were in the port. The ships had lots of goods.

Detail
The Phoenician merchants were on land. They were selling their goods .

Topic
Carthage

Detail
The merchants of Carthage were selling their goods, too.

Detail
The two groups of merchants were exchanging goods, talking, and laughing.

Photomondo/Photodisc/Getty Images

Write About the Text I used notes from my idea web to write an informative paragraph about Carthage.

Student Model: *Informative Text*

It was a busy trading day in Carthage. The Phoenician cargo ships were in the port. The ships had lots of goods. The goods included sweet grapes, olives, and wheat. They also included cedar wood and beautiful shining objects of glass. The Phoenician merchants were on land. They were selling their goods to the merchants of Carthage. The merchants of Carthage were selling their goods, too. The two groups of merchants were busy exchanging goods, laughing, and talking.

TALK ABOUT IT

COLLABORATE

Text Evidence
Draw a box around a sentence that comes from the notes. How does this detail help Isabel describe Carthage?

Grammar
Circle the past-tense verbs in the first and second sentences. Why does Isabel use the past tense to write about Carthage?

Condense Ideas
Underline the second and third sentences. How can you use the prepositional phrase *with lots of goods* to combine the sentences to condense ideas?

Your Turn
COLLABORATE

How does the author support the idea that Phoenicia was remarkable? Use text evidence.

>> *Go Digital*
Write your response online. Use your editing checklist.

TALK ABOUT IT

Essential Question

How did democracy develop?

>> Go Digital

COLLABORATE

What was this building called? What did people do there? Write words in the chart about the government of Priene.

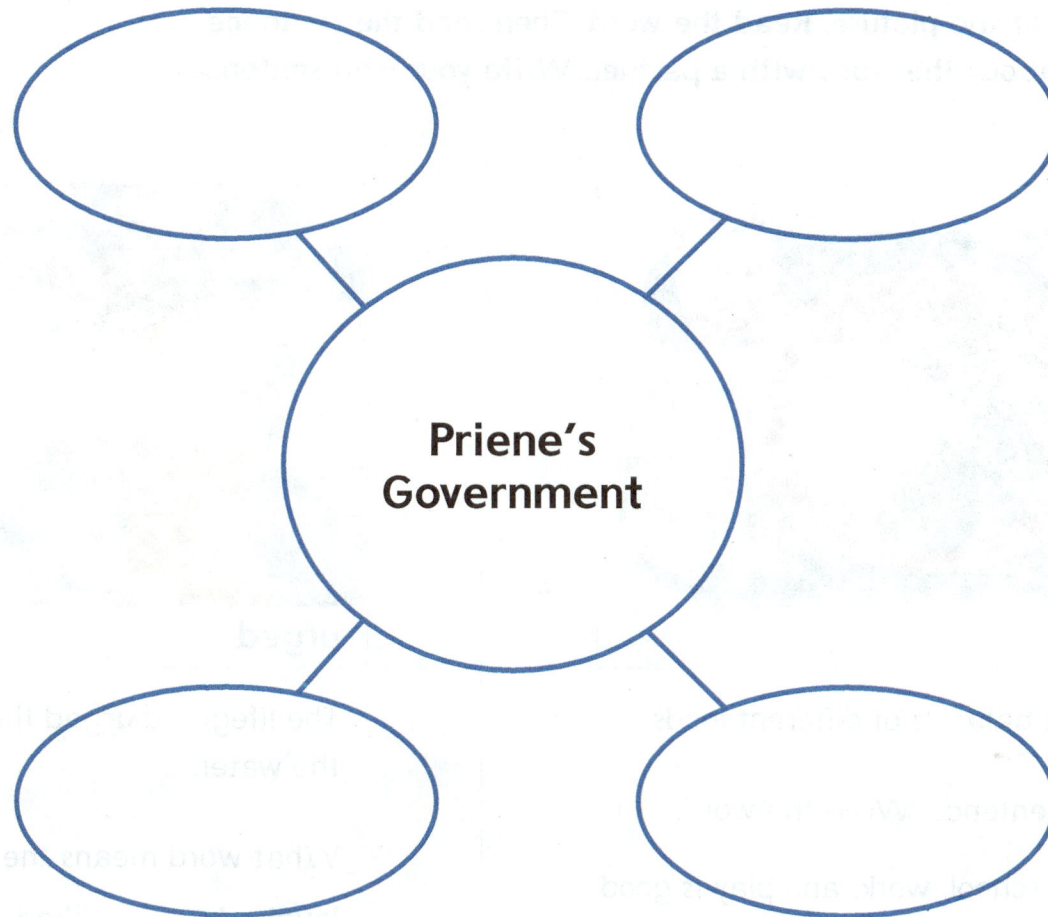

Priene's Government

Discuss the government of Priene. Use words from the chart. Complete the sentences.

The government in Priene was a _____. It had an

_____. It also had a smaller _____

council. The council met in the _____.

More Vocabulary

Look at the picture. Read the word. Then read the sentence.
Talk about the word with a partner. Write your own sentence.

balance

This meal has a **balance** of different foods.

Complete the sentence. Write the word.

A _____ of school, work, and play is good.

What do you have a balance of?

I have a balance of _____

_____.

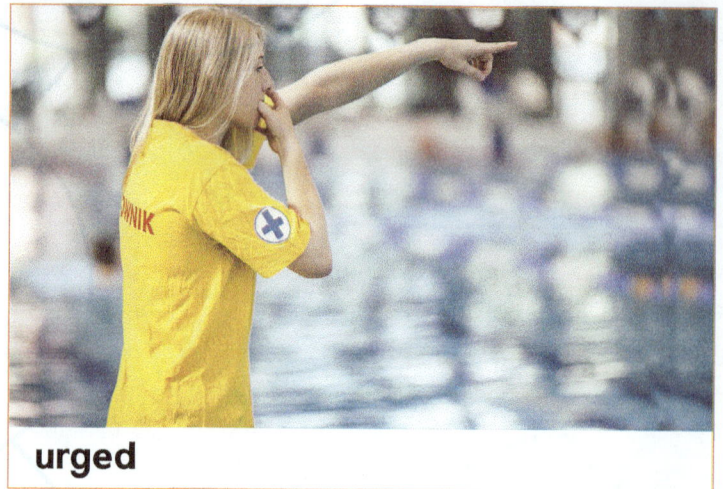

urged

The lifeguard **urged** the people to get out of the water.

What word means the same as *urged*?

laughed   **liked**   **told**

What have you urged a friend to do?

I have urged a friend to _____

_____.

Words and Phrases: Prefixes *un-* and *re-*

The prefix *un-* means "not."

unlike = not like
What season is unlike summer?
Winter is **un**like summer.

The prefix *re-* means "again."

revisit = visit again
What will the man revisit?
He will **re**visit his school.

COLLABORATE Talk with a partner. Look at the pictures. Read the sentences.
Circle the meaning of the underlined word.

The dog is unfriendly.

not friendly   **friendly again**

Lucia has to rewrite the math problems.

not write   **write again**

JP Alcaraz/Moment Open/Getty Images; WhitneyLewisPhotography/iStock/360/Getty Images; VikramRaghuvanshi/E+/Getty Images; Molly_Wolff_Photography/iStock/360/Getty Images;

COLLABORATE

❶ Talk About It

Look at the photographs. Read the title. Discuss what you see. Use these words.

democracy	debate
thinkers	ancient

Write about what you see.

The text is about _____

_____ .

What do the photos show?

The photos show _____

_____ .

What do the photos tell you about the text?

The photos _____

_____ .

Take notes as you read the text.

The Democracy DEBATE

Essential Question

? **How did democracy develop?**

Read about the ideas that philosophers in ancient Greece and Rome had about democracy.

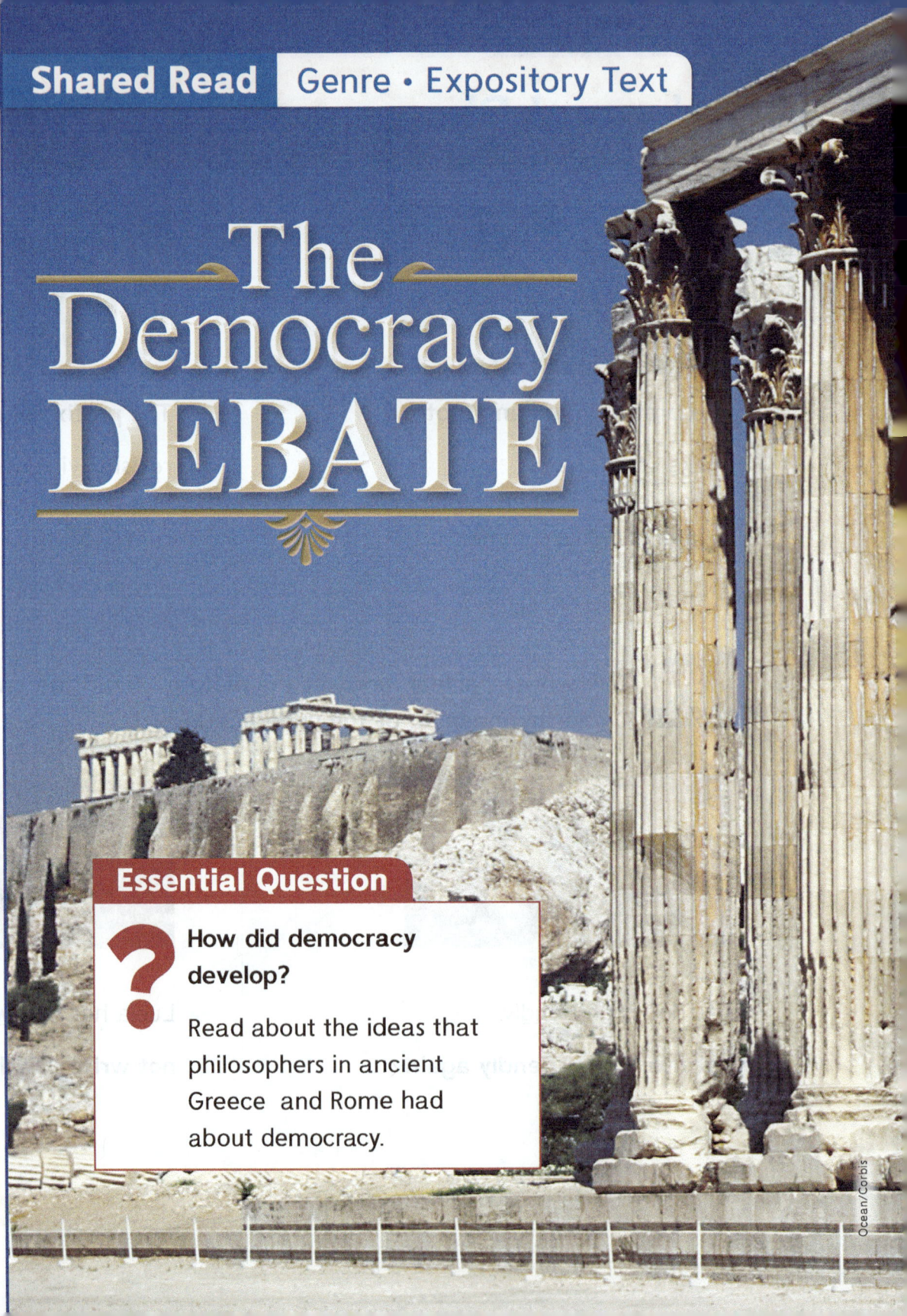

Ocean/Corbis

Born and Raised in Greece

The word *democracy* means "government by the people." The United States is a type of democracy. So are many other countries around the world. Democracy began in ancient Greece.

Even when democracy was new, people argued about how it should work. Should all people be allowed to vote? How should power be shared? Ancient Greek philosophers debated these issues.

Great Minds

The word *philosopher* means "lover of wisdom." A philosopher seeks knowledge. The Greek philosopher Socrates lived nearly 2,500 years ago. He thought deeply about democracy. He criticized the idea of a government run by all people. He felt that only fair and wise people should be allowed to decide things.

Some people in Athens were afraid of Socrates. They thought his ideas were dangerous. To keep Socrates' ideas from spreading to the youth of Athens, he was put to death.

Socrates

Students of Philosophy

The philosopher Plato had studied with Socrates. In 380 B.C. Plato published a book, *The Republic,* about government. Unlike his teacher, he believed that three different groups of people should work together in government. The highest group would be philosopher-kings. The second group would be soldiers. The third group would be common people.

Plato

(c) Siede Preis/Getty Images; (t) Lysippos/The Bridgeman Art Library/Getty Images; (b) DEA/G. DAGLI ORTI/De Agostini Picture Library/Getty Images

Text Evidence

1 Sentence Structure A C T

Read the first line of the second paragraph. Circle the pronoun *it*. Underline the noun that the pronoun *it* refers to. What did people argue about?

People argued about _____.

2 Specific Vocabulary A C T

Read the third paragraph. Draw a box around the meaning of *philosopher.* What does a philosopher seek, or want?

A philosopher seeks _____

_____

**3 Comprehension
Compare and Contrast**

Read the fifth paragraph. Socrates believed that only fair and wise men should run the government. How did Plato's ideas contrast with Socrates' ideas? Circle the sentence that tells you.

_____

21

1 Talk About It

Why didn't Aristotle believe in a government run by a few educated men?

That government would benefit

_____.

Why didn't Aristotle believe in a government run by common people?

Common people might not make

_____.

2 Specific Vocabulary Ⓐ Ⓒ Ⓣ

Reread the third sentence. *Moderation* means "not doing too much of one thing." Underline a word that means almost the same thing.

3 Sentence Structure Ⓐ Ⓒ Ⓣ

Read the third sentence of the third paragraph. Why was the Roman republic breaking down?

The Roman republic was breaking

down because _____.

Around 388 B.C., Plato formed a school called the Academy. His star student was Aristotle. Aristotle believed in balance and moderation. He believed that a government that tried to restrict power to a few educated men would not work. It would benefit only the rich. But a democracy run by common people would not work either. Such people might not make wise decisions. Aristotle wanted to combine the two. This would give people from all parts of society a voice.

Aristotle

Changes in Rome

Ancient Greece had an important influence on ancient Rome. Cicero is the best-known Roman philosopher. He lived about 400 years after Aristotle. Like Aristotle, he believed a balance of power brought peace and prosperity.

Cicero believed that the Roman republic was the best model for government. The Roman government had features of a monarchy, an aristocracy, and a democracy. The Roman republic was breaking down, however, because the aristocracy had gained too much power. In his book, Cicero urged a return to a more balanced government.

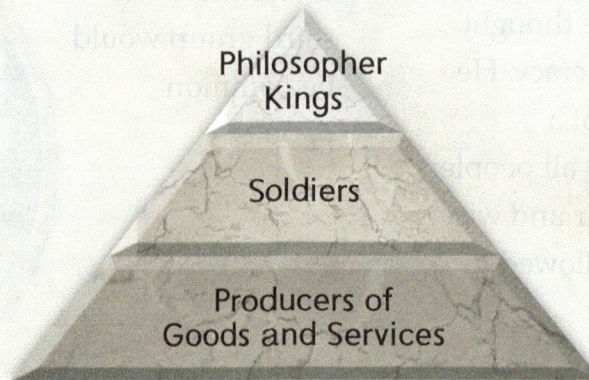

Philosopher Kings

Soldiers

Producers of Goods and Services

Cicero

Philosopher	Place	Time Period	Ideas About Democracy
Socrates	Greece	469–399 B.C.	Only wise and just people should govern.
Plato	Greece	427–347 B.C.	Rule should be shared by philosopher-kings, soldiers, and providers of goods.
Aristotle	Greece	384–322 B.C.	Educated and common people should each have a role in government.
Cicero	Rome	106–43 B.C.	The Roman republic—a monarch, an aristocracy, and the people—is best.

The Debate Continues

The founders of the United States also thought about how a democracy should be organized. They believed that they should revisit Greek and Roman ideas for their new government. Thomas Paine wrote booklets to promote the idea that people should govern themselves. James Madison admired Aristotle's and Cicero's beliefs in balancing power among different groups.

In 1787, James Madison and Alexander Hamilton wrote a set of essays called *The Federalist* to encourage states to vote for the Constitution. They wanted two law-making groups. One, the Senate, would be similar to the aristocrats of Rome. The other, the House of Representatives, would give more people a voice. They also endorsed having one president.

Today, people are still debating how to run the U.S. government. The U.S. Constitution has been amended more than 25 times. Yet it is important to remember that our government has roots in ideas from ancient times. Democracy has withstood the test of time.

Make Connections

? Talk about how the philosophers' ideas influenced our democracy. **ESSENTIAL QUESTION**

How does your understanding of democracy compare to the ideas the philosophers had? **TEXT TO SELF**

Text Evidence

❶ Comprehension
Compare and Contrast

Read the first paragraph. Like Aristotle and Cicero, how did Madison and Hamilton want to balance the government?

They wanted to balance power

among _____.

❷ Sentence Structure Ⓐ Ⓒ Ⓣ

Read the last sentence of the second paragraph. Whom does the pronoun *they* refer to?

The pronoun *they* refers to _____

_____.

COLLABORATE

❸ Talk About It

Discuss a sentence that best expresses the main idea of this text. Then write it.

_____

_____

Respond to the Text

Partner Discussion Work with a partner. Read the questions about "The Democracy Debate." Show where you found text evidence. Write the page numbers. Then discuss what you learned.

How did the Greeks think about democracy?

Socrates thought _____.

Aristotle thought _____.

Text Evidence

Page(s): _____

Page(s): _____

How did the Romans think about democracy?

Cicero thought _____.

Text Evidence

Page(s): _____

How did the founders of the United States think about democracy?

The Senate _____.

The House of Representatives _____.

The Constitution _____.

Text Evidence

Page(s): _____

Page(s): _____

Page(s): _____

Group Discussion Present your answers to the group. Cite text evidence for your ideas. Listen to and discuss the group's opinions.

Write Work with a partner. Look at your notes about "The Democracy Debate." Write your answer to the Essential Question. Use text evidence to support your answer. Use vocabulary words in your writing.

How did different groups of people think about democracy?

The Greeks thought _____

_____.

The Romans thought _____

_____.

The founders of the United States thought _____

_____.

Share Writing Present your writing to the class. Discuss their opinions. Talk about their ideas. Explain why you agree or disagree with their ideas. You can say:

I agree with _____.

That's a good comment, but _____.

Write to Sources

Kevin

Take Notes About the Text I took notes on the idea web to answer the prompt: *Pretend you are Plato. Tell why your ideas about democracy are the best. Include text evidence.*

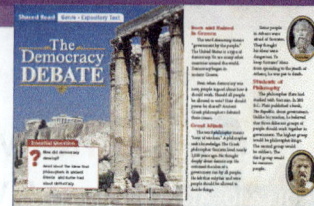

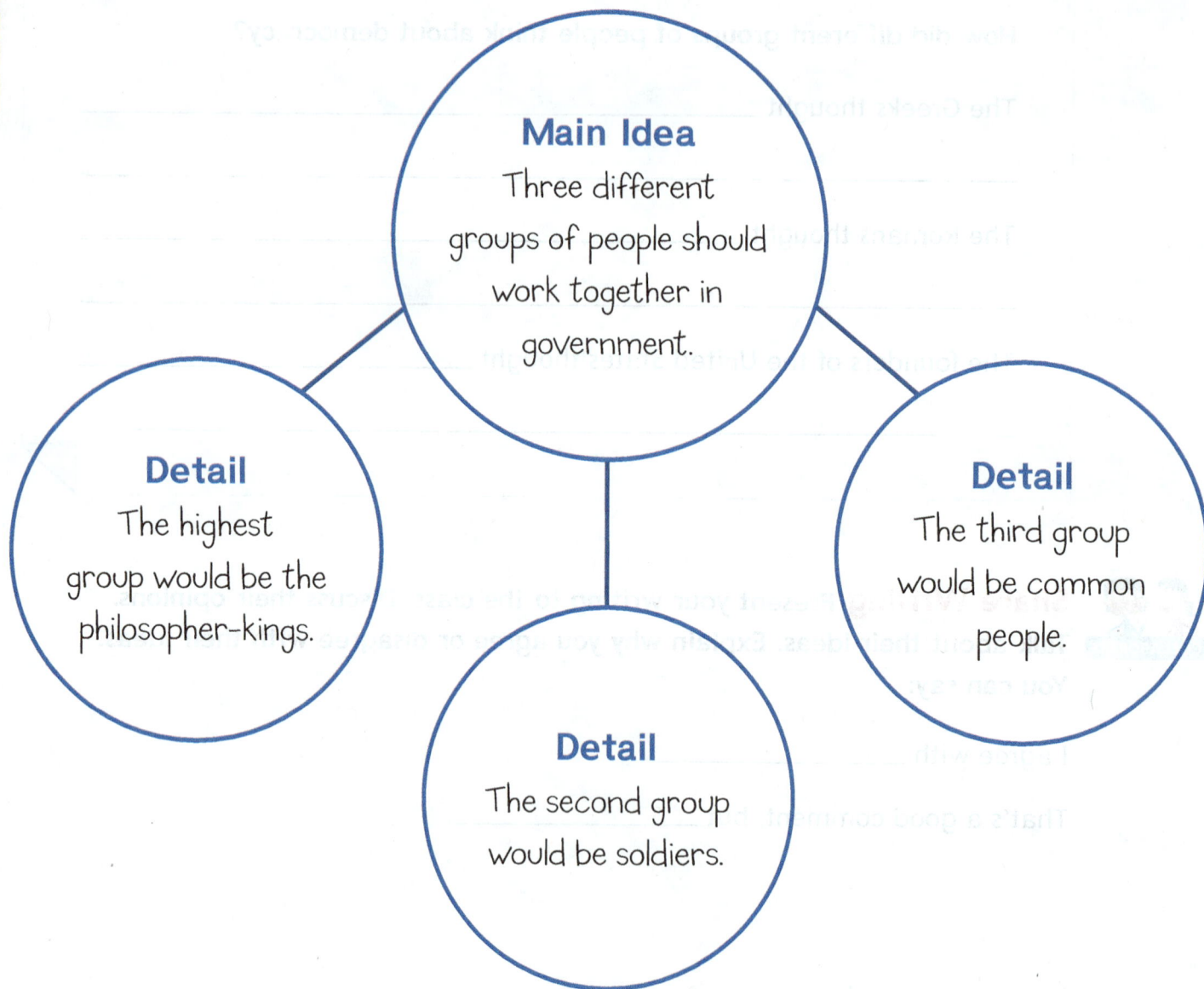

pages 20–23

Main Idea
Three different groups of people should work together in government.

Detail
The highest group would be the philosopher-kings.

Detail
The second group would be soldiers.

Detail
The third group would be common people.

Write About the Text I used notes from my idea web to write an argument.

Student Model: *Argument*

My ideas about democracy are the best. Three groups of people are important to Greece. These three groups should work together in government. The highest group would be the philosopher-kings. They are wise. The second group would be soldiers. They will protect everyone. The third group would be common people. They will do what is fair for everyone. These groups are important to Greece. They should all be a part of the government.

TALK ABOUT IT

COLLABORATE

Text Evidence

Underline a detail sentence that comes from the notes. How does this detail sentence support Kevin's argument?

Grammar

Draw a box around the pronoun *they* in the last sentence. What noun phrase in the next-to-last sentence does the pronoun refer to?

Connect Ideas

Underline the last two sentences. How can you use the word *so* to combine the sentences to connect ideas?

Your Turn

COLLABORATE

Pretend you are one of the forefathers of the United States. Tell why the proposed United States form of democracy is the best.

>> *Go Digital*
Write your response online. Use your editing checklist.

28

This woman lived in ancient Rome. What do you learn about her from the photo? Write details in the chart.

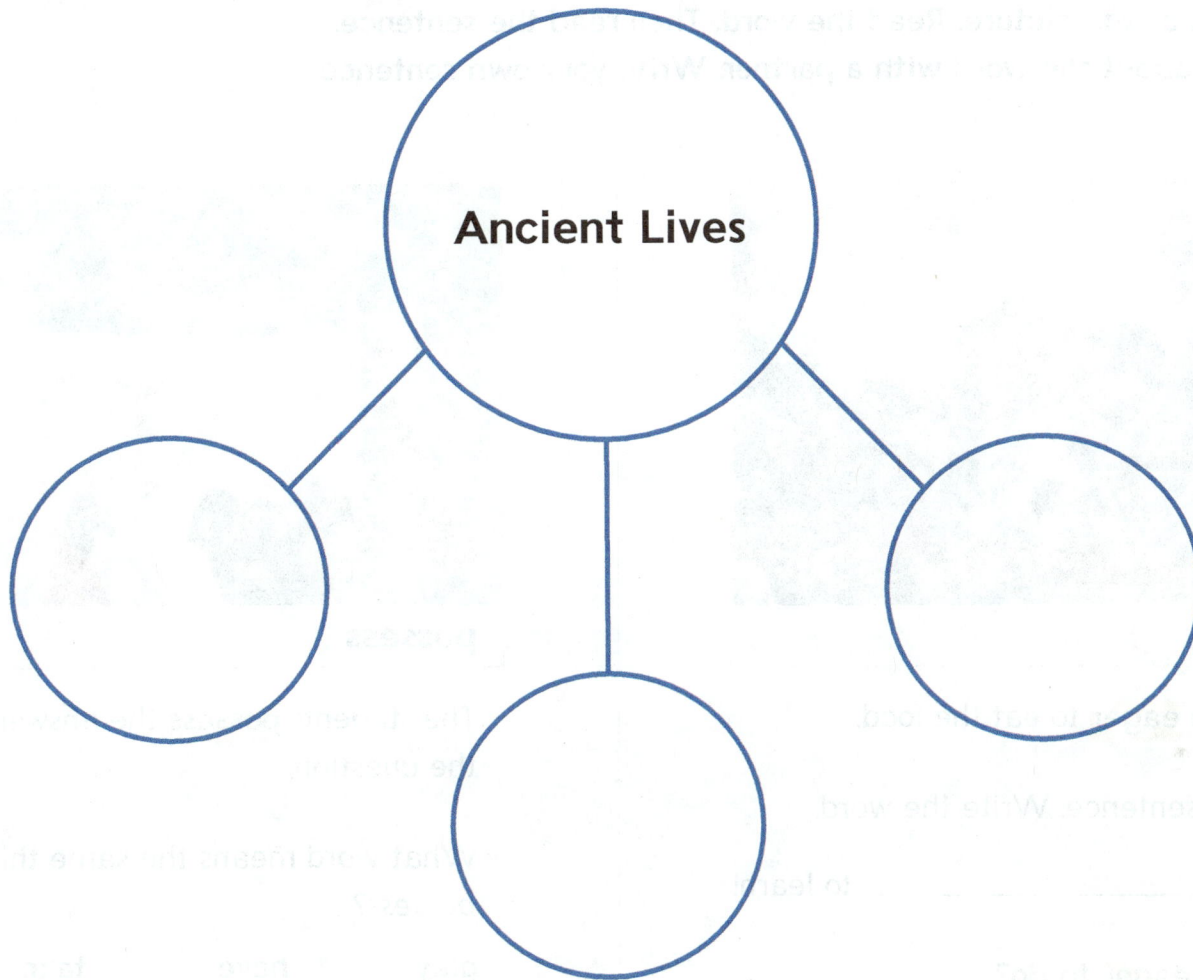

Ancient Lives

Discuss what the woman's life was like. Use words from the chart. Complete the sentences.

The woman played the _____. She wore gold _____

and nice _____.

More Vocabulary

Look at the picture. Read the word. Then read the sentence.
Talk about the word with a partner. Write your own sentence.

eager

The friends are **eager** to eat the food.

Complete the sentence. Write the word.

Our class is _____ to learn!

What are you eager to do?

I am eager to _____.

possess

The students **possess** the answer to the question.

What word means the same thing as *possess*?

play   **have**   **take**

What skill do you possess?

I possess the skill to _____.

Words and Phrases: Comparative and Superlative Adjectives

Use *-er* when comparing two people, places, or things.

Which shoes are finer?

The dress shoes are fin**er** than the gym shoes.

Use *-est* when comparing three or more people, places, or things.

Who is the oldest?

The person in the middle is the old**est**.

COLLABORATE **Talk with a partner. Look at the pictures. Read the sentences. Write the word that completes the sentence.**

The woman on the right is the

_____.

older   oldest

The gray jacket is _____ than the blue jacket.

finer   finest

31

COLLABORATE

1 Talk About It

Look at the illustration. Read the title. Discuss what you see. Use these words.

trade man boy blue stones

Write about what you see.

This story is about _____

_____.

Who are the people you see?

The people are _____

_____.

What is the man holding?

The man is holding _____

_____.

Take notes as you read the story.

Yaskul's Mighty Trade

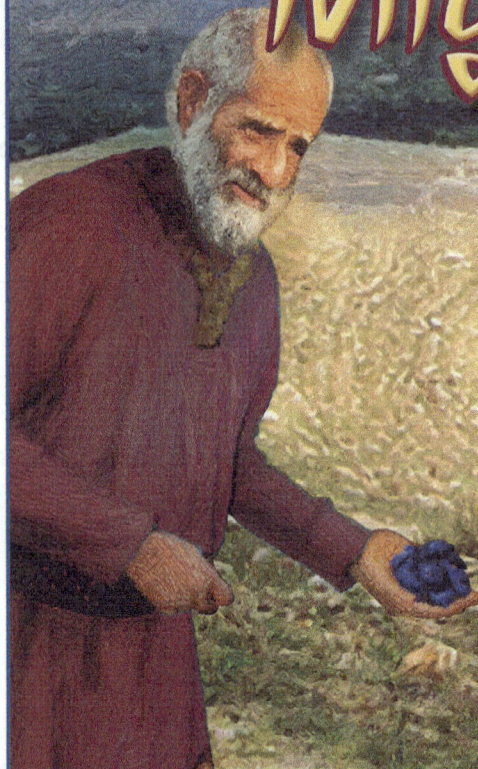

Essential Question

? What was life like for people in ancient cultures?

Read about the importance of trade on the Silk Road in the ancient city of Bactra.

Winson Trang

The ancient city of Bactra in the Kushan Empire was a key market for merchants traveling along the Silk Road trade route. In A.D. 110, merchants from east and west traveled to the famous market in Bactra. In the following story, Yaskul, the twelve-year-old son of a Bactran merchant, is eager to make his first real trade.

I Make Plans

It is early, but I am awake. It is a cold autumn day. I think about the Chinese caravan that arrived last night. If winter comes early, my family and I may not see another caravan for months. My family must have success at the market tomorrow.

Tomorrow, I become a trader. Father says I will only watch and learn. Grandfather says that Father is too cautious. He says Father makes timid trades. And he does not get the best prices for lapis lazuli.

Lapis lazuli! I love this blue stone. Grandfather gave me some lazuli stones of my own. He is teaching me how to trade them.

Thieves!

When Grandfather and I reach our storage room today, Father is already there. "Thieves!" he cries. "They took everything!" Grandfather looks around the room and says they did not take everything.

Text Evidence

1 Sentence Structure A C T

Read the third sentence in the Introduction. How old is the boy in this story? Circle the words that tell you.

2 Specific Vocabulary A C T

Read the third sentence of the first paragraph. The word *caravan* means "a group of people and animals traveling together through a desert." How do you know the caravan is a moving thing?

I know the caravan is a moving thing because the sentence says

that it _____.

3 Comprehension
Point of View

Read the second sentence of the second paragraph. Who is telling this story? Whom does the pronoun *I* refer to? Draw a box around the name in the Introduction.

Text Evidence

1 Sentence Structure ⒶⒸⓉ

Read the first sentence. Circle the words that tell who is speaking. What did the thieves take?

Father says that the thieves took

_____ .

2 Specific Vocabulary ⒶⒸⓉ

Reread the first paragraph. Underline a context clue for the word *beads*. What does Yaskul tell his father about his lazuli beads?

Yaskul tells his father _____

_____ .

COLLABORATE

3 Talk About It

Why is Yaskul nervous about trading his beads? Discuss with a partner. Then write your ideas.

Yaskul is nervous because _____

_____

_____ .

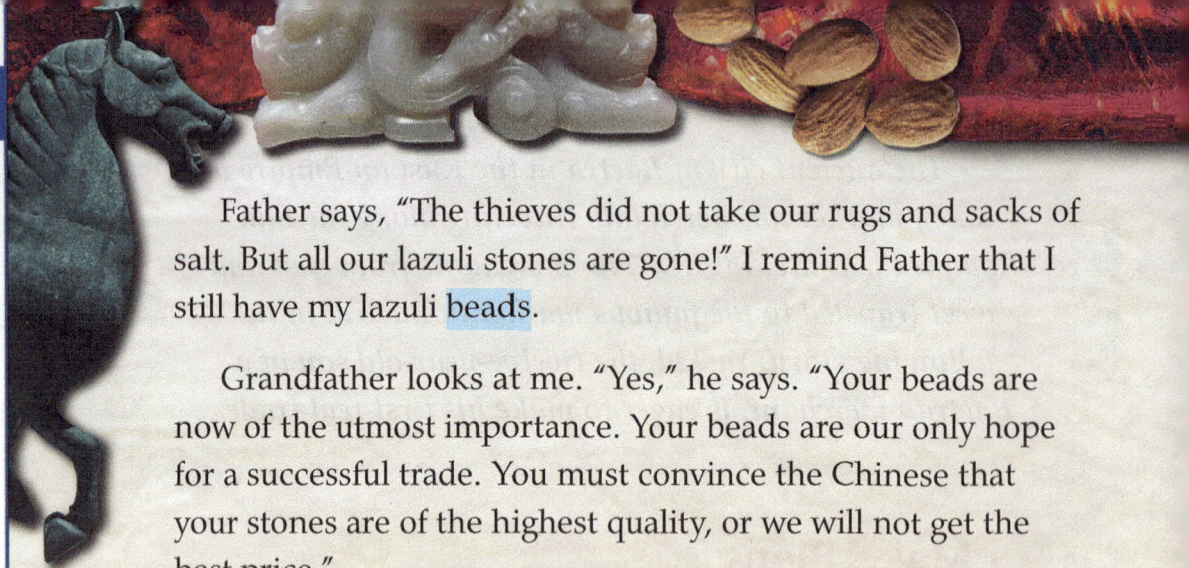

Father says, "The thieves did not take our rugs and sacks of salt. But all our lazuli stones are gone!" I remind Father that I still have my lazuli beads.

Grandfather looks at me. "Yes," he says. "Your beads are now of the utmost importance. Your beads are our only hope for a successful trade. You must convince the Chinese that your stones are of the highest quality, or we will not get the best price."

I am nervous. Grandfather smiles and puts his hand on my shoulder. "Don't worry, Yaskul. You possess the skill to make this trade a mighty one."

I Make a Friend

In the evening, I observe the Chinese traders. Their exotic robes glow with color. Their robes are much finer than my clothes.

Suddenly, one man about 19 years old walks toward me. I jump back, but he smiles and waves at me. "Do not be afraid." The man's voice is friendly, and he speaks my language. "Are you a trader?" he asks me.

"I am Yaskul," I say. "My family are traders." He tells me his name is Zhang.

(bkgd) Winson Trang; (tl) TAO Images/SuperStock; (tc) PASCAL PAVANI/Staff/AFP/Getty Images; (tr) Stockbyte/Getty Images; (r) PjrStudio/Alamy

I tell him that thieves stole our goods. "You have had bad luck, but you will trade well," Zhang says. I hope he is right.

Trading Day

I make my beads into a necklace to show off the stones. Father guards our remaining goods all night. In the morning, we transport the goods to the marketplace.

We reach our stall as the Chinese traders arrive. Zhang nods to me as Father begins talking with the oldest Chinese trader. He does not seem impressed by our goods.

Then Zhang speaks. "Do you have any of those beautiful blue stones?" I hold out my necklace. I notice the oldest trader's eyes light up. I tell him how fine these beads are. He agrees to pay a high price for the necklace.

Zhang winks at me. He does not say a word. After the Chinese traders depart, Grandfather hugs me. Father pats me on the back. Finally, I can call myself a trader!

Stockbyte/Getty Images

Make Connections

? Talk about the importance of trade in the lives of people living in the ancient city of Bactra. **ESSENTIAL QUESTION**

When did you overcome nervousness to succeed at something important to you? **TEXT TO SELF**

Text Evidence

1 Comprehension Point of View

Read the second paragraph. Circle the pronouns that tell you the story is written from the first-person point of view.

2 Sentence Structure ACT

Read the first sentence of the third paragraph. Circle the word *as*. The word *as* shows that two things happen at the same time. Underline the two things that happen at the same time.

3 Specific Vocabulary ACT

Read the fourth sentence in the fourth paragraph. The idiom *eyes light up* means "eyes look happy or excited." When do the oldest trader's eyes light up?

His eyes light up when _____

_____

_____.

Respond to the Text

Partner Discussion Work with a partner. Read the questions about "Yaskul's Mighty Trade." Show where you found text evidence. Write the page numbers. Then discuss what you read.

Where did Yaskul and his family live?

Yaskul and his family lived _____.   **Text Evidence** 🔍
Page(s): _____

Bactra was _____.   Page(s): _____

Caravans come from places such as _____ to trade in Bactra.   Page(s): _____

What did Yaskul and his family trade?

Yaskul's family traded _____.   **Text Evidence** 🔍
Page(s): _____

But the night before the market, _____.   Page(s): _____

Yaskul's stones are important because _____

_____.   Page(s): _____

Group Discussion Present your answers to the group. Cite text evidence for your ideas. Listen to and discuss the group's opinions.

Write Work with a partner. Look at your notes about "Yaskul's Mighty Trade." Write your answer to the Essential Question. Use text evidence to support your answer. Use vocabulary words in your writing.

COLLABORATE

> **Why was trade important to Yaskul and his family?**
>
> Bactra _____.
>
> Yaskul's family traded _____.
>
> Trade was important to Yaskul and his family because _____
>
> _____.

Share Writing Present your writing to the class. Discuss their opinions. Talk about their ideas. Explain why you agree or disagree with their ideas. You can say:

COLLABORATE

I agree with _____.

That is a good comment, but _____.

Write to Sources

Take Notes About the Text I took notes on the sequence chart to answer the prompt: *Write about Yaskul's next trade in which he sells a rug to a trader and gets a high price. Use the first-person point of view and include dialogue.*

pages 32–35

Paige

First
Yaskul makes beads into a necklace to show off the stones.

Next
He holds out the necklace.

Then
Yaskul tells the oldest trader how fine the beads are.

Last
The trader agrees to pay a high price for the necklace.

Write About the Text I used notes from my sequence chart to write about Yaskul's next trade.

Student Model: *Narrative Text*

Three traders walk up to our stall. They look at the rugs we have for sale. I point to a large rug. I notice that one of the traders is interested.

"Do you want to see this fine rug?" I ask.

"I do," he says.

He looks at the rug. I tell him how fine the rug is. He agrees to pay a high price for the rug. I make my second successful trade!

TALK ABOUT IT

Text Evidence

Underline a sentence that comes from the notes. Why is this event likely to happen in Yaskul's next trade?

Grammar

Draw a box around the adjective that describes the rug in the second paragraph. Why does Paige use this adjective in the story?

Dialogue

Underline the dialogue. What is the purpose of using dialogue in a story?

Your Turn

Add an event to the story in which Yaskul and Zhang talk to each other after Yaskul sells the beads. Use details from the story.

>> Go Digital
Write your response online. Use your editing checklist.

? **Essential Question**
What influences the
development of a culture?

>> *Go Digital*

Look at the photo. How do the people farm on the mountain? Write words in the chart about what you see.

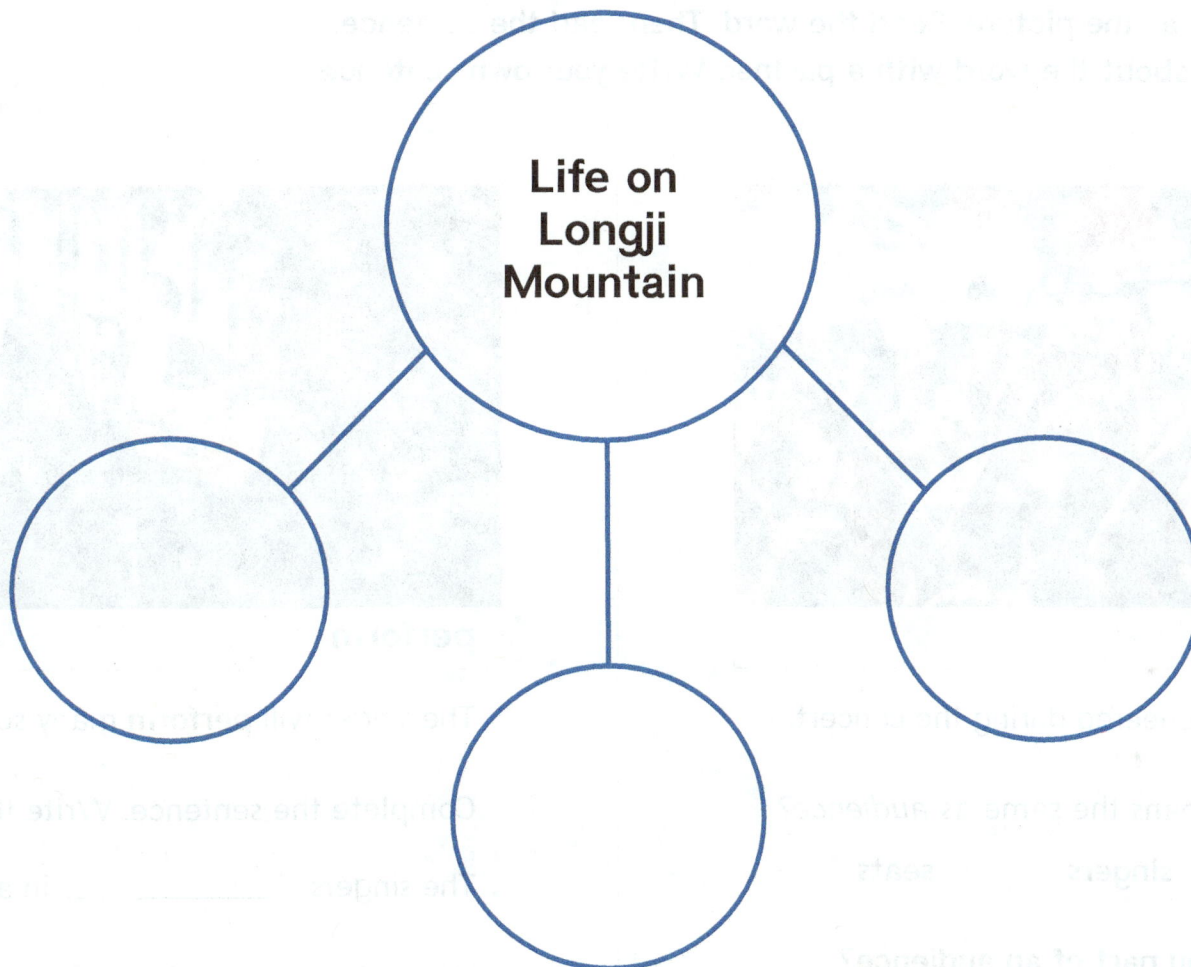

Life on
Longji
Mountain

Discuss how the land affects farming on Longji Mountain. Use words from the chart. Complete the sentences.

The farmers are growing _____. They cut _____

into the mountain. They _____ the fields with water.

More Vocabulary

COLLABORATE Look at the picture. Read the word. Then read the sentence.
Talk about the word with a partner. Write your own sentence.

audience

The **audience** cheered during the concert.

What word means the same as *audience*?

people   singers   seats

When were you part of an audience?

I was part of an audience at _____

_____.

perform

The singer will **perform** many songs.

Complete the sentence. Write the word.

The singers _____ in a concert.

What do you want to perform in?

I want to perform in a _____.

momcilog/iStock/Getty Images Plus/Getty Images; Comstock Images/SuperStock

42

Words and Phrases: *your, our*

The word *your* tells what belongs to you.

What do you like?

You like **your** new bicycle.

The word *our* tells what belongs to us.

What are we doing?

We are reading **our** books.

COLLABORATE

Talk with a partner. Look at the pictures. Read the sentences. Write the word that completes the sentence.

You need _____ pen.

      your   **our**

We are playing _____ favorite game.

      your   **our**

COLLABORATE

1 Talk About It

Look at the illustration. Read the title. Discuss what you see. Use these words.

secret girl woman weaving

Write about what you see.

The story is about _____

_____.

Who are the people you see?

The people are _____

_____.

What is the girl doing?

The girl is _____

_____.

Take notes as you read the story.

Cusi's Secret

Janet Broxon

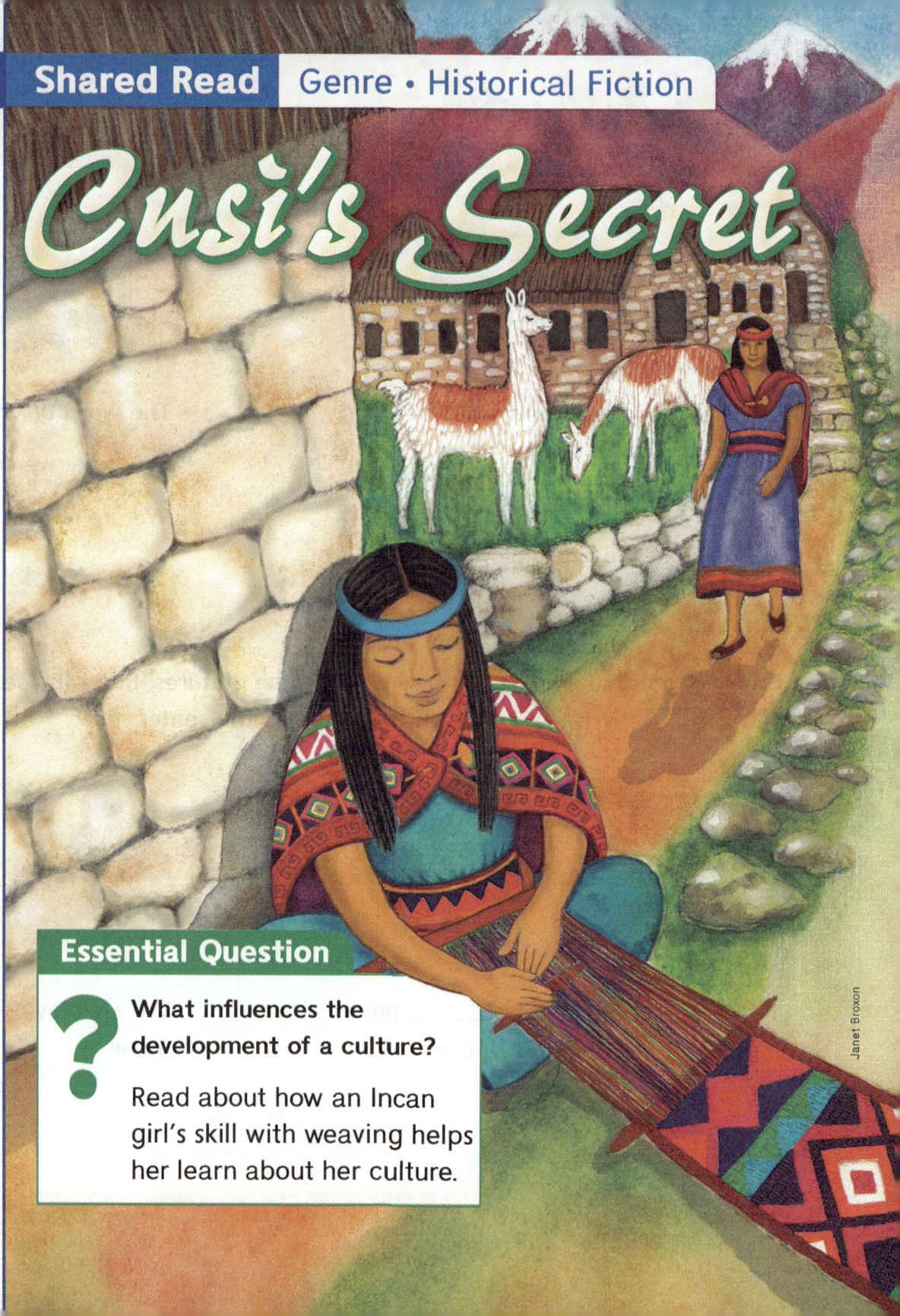

Essential Question

?

What influences the development of a culture?

Read about how an Incan girl's skill with weaving helps her learn about her culture.

The Inca value beautiful textiles, or cloth. The year is 1430, and Cusi is an 11-year-old Incan girl with a special talent for weaving. Although few girls are allowed to receive an education in Incan society, Cusi dreams of going to school.

Learning from Family

Cusi and her mother worked at their handheld looms. Cusi asked, "Mama, how did our family become such fine weavers?"

"I learned how to weave from *my* mother, your grandmother," Cusi's mother said. "Your grandmother learned from her mother, too."

Cusi gazed over at the girls' schoolhouse on a nearby hill. "How I wish I could go there," Cusi said. "Why do so few girls have a chance to learn?"

School

Cusi saw one of the school's *mamaconas*, or teachers, walking along a nearby path. The woman stopped to watch Cusi weave. Cusi pretended not to see the teacher. But she did her very best to show off her skills.

Cusi's hands glided over the woolen strands, darting as quickly as a hummingbird flies. The teacher watched in amazement.

Then Cusi looked up to see her parents greeting the teacher at the door. The teacher talked to them. "I watched your daughter working at her loom. She is young to have such expertise. Will you allow her to become one of my students?"

ILLUSTRATIONS: Janet Broxon

Text Evidence

1 Specific Vocabulary Ⓐ Ⓒ Ⓣ

Read the second sentence in the Introduction. The word *talent* means "a natural ability to do something well." What is Cusi's talent?

Cusi has a talent for _____.

2 Comprehension
Point of View

Read the first paragraph. Circle the nouns and pronouns that tell you the story is told from the third-person point of view. What does Cusi want to know? Underline the question.

3 Sentence Structure Ⓐ Ⓒ Ⓣ

Read the third paragraph. Who is speaking? Underline the words that tell you. Where does Cusi wish she could go?

Cusi wishes she could go to the

_____.

45

❶ Comprehension
Point of View

Read the first sentence. Circle the nouns and pronouns that tell you the story is written from the third-person point of view. Why didn't Cusi "jump for joy"? Underline the words that tell you.

COLLABORATE

❷ Talk About It

What does Cusi learn at school? Discuss with a partner. Then write about it.

At school, Cusi learns _____

_____

_____.

❸ Specific Vocabulary Ⓐ Ⓒ Ⓣ

Read the last sentence of the fifth paragraph. The verb *fascinated* means "interested someone very much." What fascinated Cusi?

The _____
fascinated Cusi.

Cusi wanted to jump for joy, but she knew she couldn't **display** her emotions. Cusi's father said, "We would be honored to have Cusi attend school. An education will be of great benefit to her."

Cusi felt hopeful. But she was nervous, too.

Learning at School

Cusi found living at the school so different from being at home. She learned about Incan history and beliefs. She also learned how to prepare foods.

The highlight of Cusi's new life was weaving class. She loved learning to spin yarn from the wool of *vicuñas*. Cusi had seen the tiny camels roaming distant hills. Once on market day, she had even secretly stroked a garment made from their silky wool. Cusi knew only royal people could wear such robes.

One afternoon, Cusi began to daydream in class. She remembered the time she had seen a village elder using a *quipu*. He used it to count the alpacas in the herds. The counting tool, made by knotting strands of wool, **fascinated** her.

Cusi had asked the man how to use the counting threads. The man had shouted angrily at Cusi. "Only men may use the *quipu!*"

Cusi had run away. But she never forgot about the *quipu*. Even now, her fingers worked at tying knots in a wool cord. She knew the *quipu* was a key to great knowledge.

A classmate's shout startled Cusi from her thoughts. "Cusi fell asleep!" The girls broke into laughter. Cusi hid the knots in her lap.

"Enough!" the teacher said to quiet the class. "Cusi, please step outside."

Keeping a Secret

Cusi held the knotted wool behind her back. "Show me what you have made," Mamacona said sternly. Cusi gave her the knots. "Is this a *quipu*? Women should not have these things."

"But if I knew how to use the *quipu*," Cusi pleaded, "I could keep school records. Then the royal merchants could no longer cheat us when buying our *vicuña* robes."

Mamacona had also had a thirst for knowledge when she was a girl. Her brother had secretly taught her how to keep accounts with the *quipu*.

"I will teach you how to make a *quipu*," she whispered. Cusi's face lit up. "But you must promise never to tell anyone!"

Cusi hugged her teacher. "I promise. I will learn, and I will forever keep our secret!"

Make Connections

? Talk about the importance of wool and weaving in the Incan culture. **ESSENTIAL QUESTION**

Describe a time when you learned something you had wanted to know for a long time. **TEXT TO SELF**

Text Evidence

1 Sentence Structure (A)(C)(T)

Read the first paragraph. Circle the punctuation marks that show you someone is speaking. What did Cusi's classmate shout?

Her classmate shouted,

"_____!"

2 Specific Vocabulary (A)(C)(T)

Read the first sentence of the fifth paragraph. The idiom *a thirst for knowledge* means "a desire to know." Who had also had a thirst for knowledge when she was a girl?

_____

COLLABORATE

3 Talk About It

What does Mamacona agree to do at the end of the story? What does Cusi promise to do?

Mamacona agrees to _____.

Cusi promises to _____.

47

Respond to the Text

Partner Discussion Work with a partner. Read the questions about "Cusi's Secret." Show where you found text evidence. Write the page numbers. Then discuss what you read.

Why is Cusi invited to attend school?

A teacher from the girls' school _____.

Cusi does her best to _____.

The teacher is amazed. She _____.

Text Evidence 🔍

Page(s): _____

Page(s): _____

Page(s): _____

What does Cusi learn about her culture?

Cusi learns about _____ at school.

Cusi wants to learn _____.

Mamacona agrees _____.

Text Evidence 🔍

Page(s): _____

Page(s): _____

Page(s): _____

Group Discussion Present your answers to the group. Cite text evidence for your ideas. Listen to and discuss the group's opinions.

48

Write Work with a partner. Look at your notes about "Cusi's Secret." Write your answer to the Essential Question. Use text evidence to support your answer. Use vocabulary words in your writing.

How does Cusi learn about her culture?

A teacher from the girls' school watches _____

and _____.

Cusi learns about _____ at school.

Cusi is able to learn about her culture because _____

_____.

Share Writing Present your writing to the class. Discuss their opinions. Talk about their ideas. Explain why you agree or disagree with their ideas. You can say:

I agree with _____.

That's a good comment, but _____.

Write to Sources

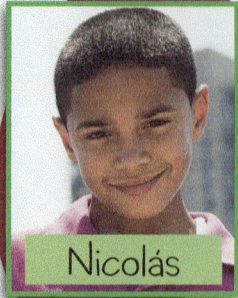

Nicolás

Take Notes About the Text I took notes on the idea web to answer the prompt: *Write a paragraph from Mamacona's point of view. Tell how she feels about teaching Cusi how to use a quipu.*

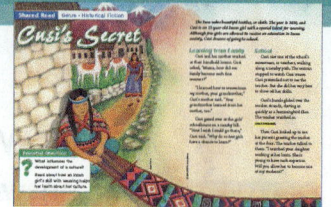

pages 44–47

Detail
Mamacona had also had a thirst for knowledge when she was a girl.

Detail
Her brother had secretly taught her to keep accounts with the quipu.

Topic
Mamacona

Detail
Mamacona wants to teach Cusi how to make a quipu.

Detail
Cusi must not tell anyone else.

50

Write About the Text I used notes from my idea web to write a paragraph from Mamacona's point of view.

Student Model: *Narrative Text*

It is a risk to teach Cusi how to use a quipu. I wanted to say no. I almost did. Then I remembered something. I had had a thirst for knowledge when I was a girl, too. My brother had secretly taught me to keep accounts with the quipu. Today, this skill helps me at work. I want to help Cusi learn this skill, too. I know she will not tell anyone else. She will keep the secret. I have decided to take the risk to help Cusi.

TALK ABOUT IT

COLLABORATE

Text Evidence
Draw a box around a sentence that comes from the notes. Why does Nicolás use this detail in his paragraph?

Grammar
Circle a present-tense verb. Why does Nicolás use this present-tense verb in his paragraph?

Connect Ideas
Underline the last two sentences. How can you use the word *so* to combine the sentences to connect ideas?

Your Turn

COLLABORATE

Write a paragraph from Cusi's point of view. Tell what she will do the next time she sells vicuña robes to the royal merchants. Use text evidence.

>> *Go Digital*
Write your response online. Use your editing checklist.

51

? **Essential Question**
What can the past teach us?

>> Go Digital

The people are standing in a temple. What questions could they ask about the temple? Write the questions in the chart.

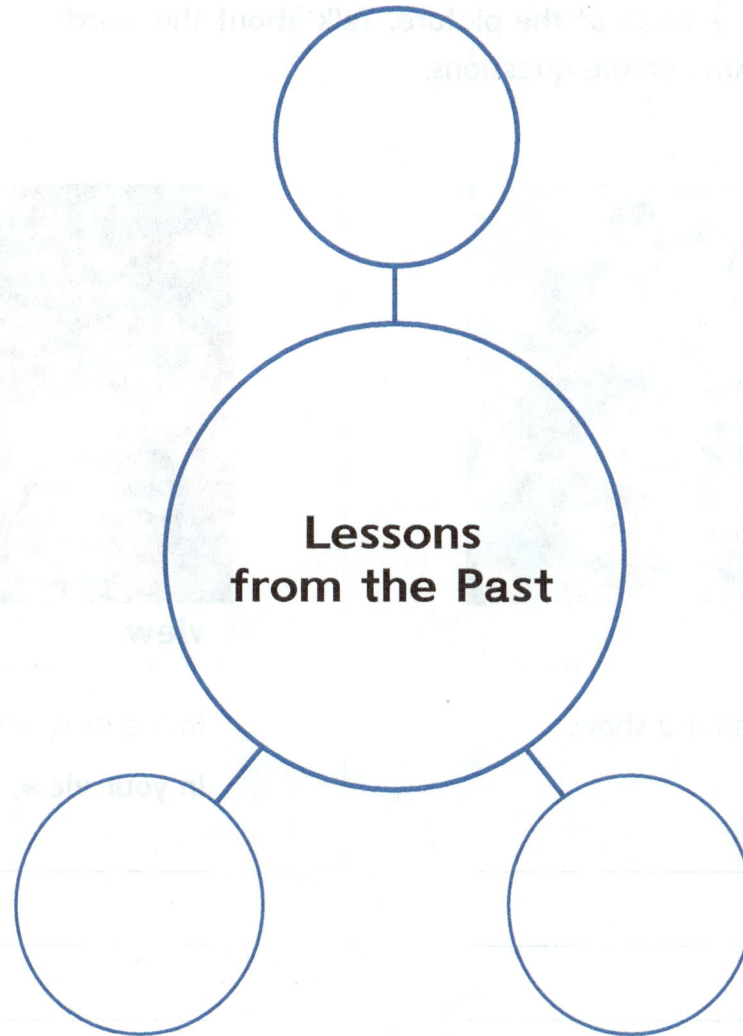

Lessons from the Past

Discuss how the temple makes us think about the past. Use words from the chart. You can say:

The temple makes us ask _____.

More Vocabulary

Read the sentence. Look at the picture. Talk about the word
with a partner. Answer the questions.

create

The students **create** posters for a show.

What can you create?

_____

_____

_____

view

In the girls' **view**, the party is exciting.

In your view, what thing is exciting?

_____

_____

_____

Poetry Terms

rhyme scheme

Some poems have rhyming words at the end of lines. This is called a rhyme scheme. Rhyme schemes can have different patterns.

Cats and kittens express their views
With hisses, purrs, and little mews.
Instead of taking baths like me,
They use their tongues quite handily.

The pattern of rhyme in this poem is *aabb*. The letters show which lines rhyme.

aa = *views* and *mews*

bb = *me* and *handily*

personification

When a writer uses personification, the writer gives a human ability—such as laughing—to something that is not human—such as an animal.

Hey diddle, diddle
The cat and the fiddle
The cow jumped over the moon;
The little dog laughed
To see such sport
And the dish ran away with the spoon.

COLLABORATE

Work with a partner. Read the poem together. Then complete the sentence. Underline the correct answer.

When danger is very near,
The shy turtle doesn't fear.
He pulls in his head and feet
And he's gone. How very neat!

The use of the word

_____

shows personification.

shy   danger   gone

COLLABORATE

❶ Talk About It

Discuss the first and second stanzas with a partner. Where did the speaker work as a boy? What did he learn how to make?

The speaker worked at _____

_____.

He learned how to make _____.

❷ Literary Element

Rhyme Scheme

Reread the first stanza. Circle the word that rhymes with *ten*. Draw a box around the word that rhymes with *took*.

❸ Specific Vocabulary A C T

Read the last line of the second stanza. The phrase *raged at* means "showed anger toward someone by behaving or speaking in a certain way." Who raged at the speaker?

_____ raged at the speaker.

Lifelong Friends

When I was but a lad of ten,
I joined the world of working men,
Apprentice was the name I took,
I learned the way to print a book.

The print shop had an air of gloom,
And sunlight seemed to shun the room,
My master was a man I feared,
He raged at me and pulled his beard.

The printing press was friend to me,
Majestic as a mighty tree,
And so I grew to love that place,
My heart would sing, my pulse would race.

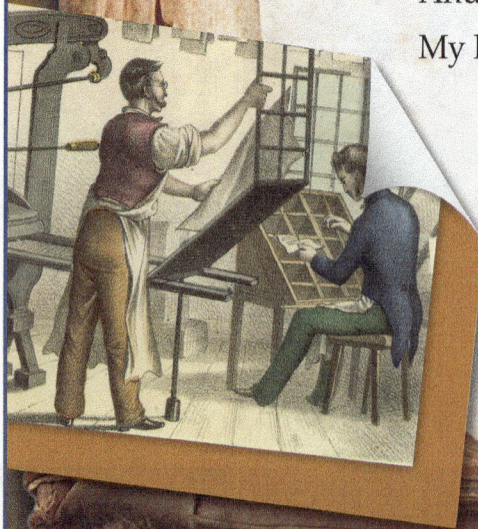

(bkgd) Michael Betts/Photographer's Choice/Getty Images; (tl) Tetra Images/Getty Images; (c) p72/Alamy; (bl) Hulton Archive/Stringer/Getty Images

Essential Question

? **What can the past teach us?**

Read what a poet learns from the past.

Each time I worked with type and ink,
I always trembled just to think
That all those many rows of words
Would soon fly up and out like birds.

Those books were tutors glad to share
Their words with people everywhere,
So many books for eager hands,
For rich and poor in many lands.

Though now my youth has passed away,
And near the hearth I spend my day,
When I'm forlorn, I contemplate
The many books I helped create.

As I commemorate my past,
One view of mine will always last:
Each book a lifelong friend might be
To someone, yes, but most to me.

—Constance Andrea Keremes

Make Connections

? How does the past affect the speaker of the poem? ESSENTIAL QUESTION

How could thinking about the past affect you in the present? TEXT TO SELF

Text Evidence

1 **Literary Element**
Personification

Read the second stanza on this page. What words does the poet use to personify the books? Circle the words.

2 **Comprehension**
Theme

Read the third stanza on this page. What does the speaker think about when he is forlorn, or sad? Write the lines that tell you.

_____

_____

COLLABORATE

3 **Talk About It**

Discuss why the speaker describes the books he helped create as "lifelong friends."

The books are lifelong friends

because _____

_____.

Respond to the Text

Partner Discussion Work with a partner. Read the questions about "Lifelong Friends." Show where you found text evidence. Write the page numbers. Then discuss what you read.

COLLABORATE

What did the speaker do in the past?

The speaker worked _____.

He learned how to print _____.

He feared _____, but he loved

_____.

Text Evidence 🔍

Page(s): _____

Page(s): _____

Page(s): _____

What does the speaker do in the present?

The speaker thinks about _____.

Thinking about these books helps the speaker when _____.

Each book is _____

to him.

Text Evidence 🔍

Page(s): _____

Page(s): _____

Page(s): _____

Group Discussion Present your answers to the group. Cite text evidence for your ideas. Listen to and discuss the group's opinions.

COLLABORATE

Write Work with a partner. Look at your notes about "Lifelong Friends." Write your answer to the Essential Question. Use text evidence to support your answer. Use vocabulary words in your writing.

> **What does the speaker learn from the past?**
>
> The speaker worked _____. He made
>
> _____.
>
> Each book is _____ to him.
>
> The speaker learns that _____.

Share Writing Present your writing to the class. Discuss their opinions. Talk about their ideas. Explain why you agree or disagree with their ideas. You can say:

I agree with _____.

That's a good comment, but _____.

Write to Sources

Brianna

Take Notes About the Text I took notes on this idea web to answer the question: *How does the poet of "Lifelong Friends" use personification to describe ordinary objects in new ways?*

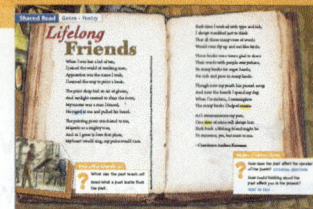

pages 56–57

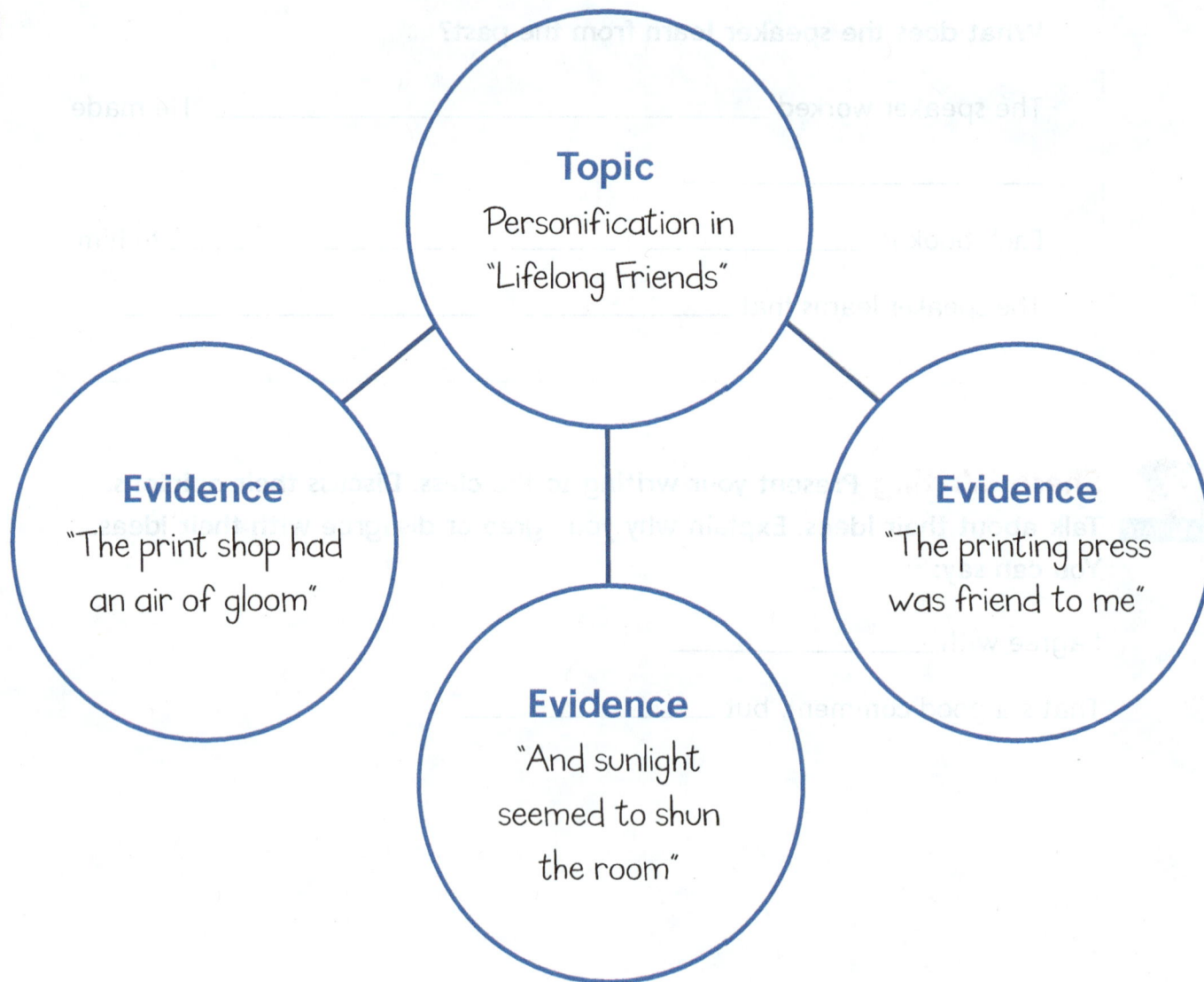

Topic
Personification in "Lifelong Friends"

Evidence
"The print shop had an air of gloom"

Evidence
"The printing press was friend to me"

Evidence
"And sunlight seemed to shun the room"

Write About the Text I used notes from my idea web to write an informative paragraph about personification in "Lifelong Friends."

Student Model: *Informative Text*

The poet of "Lifelong Friends" uses personification to describe ordinary objects in new ways. First, the poet writes, "The print shop had an air of gloom." This description helps the reader see the shop as a person filled with gloom. Next, the poet writes, "And sunlight seemed to shun the room." This description helps the reader see sunlight as a person. This person is avoiding the room. These two descriptions help the reader see ordinary objects in new ways.

TALK ABOUT IT

COLLABORATE

Text Evidence

Underline a sentence that comes from the notes. Why does Brianna use this detail in her paragraph?

Grammar

Circle *first* in the second sentence and *next* in the fourth sentence. Why does Brianna use these words?

Condense Ideas

Underline the fifth and sixth sentences. How can you use the word *who* to combine the sentences to condense ideas?

Your Turn

COLLABORATE

Write a paragraph that tells how the poet of "Lifelong Friends" uses personification to describe books.

>> *Go Digital*
Write your response online. Use your editing checklist.